SATURDAY EVENINGS
AT MENDHAM

Conversations with Madame Ouspensky

SATURDAY EVENINGS
AT MENDHAM

CONVERSATIONS WITH MADAME OUSPENSKY

Compiled and edited by
DOROTHY DARLINGTON

GURDJIEFF HERITAGE SOCIETY

Gurdjieff Heritage Society

TABLE OF CONTENTS

PREFACE

Madame Ouspensky's place in Gurdjieff's System is relatively unknown. Her role was never publicized. People on the periphery were not even aware that her House in the country existed.

Madame and P. D. Ouspensky had both very specific functions in the work. His was to disseminate the Ideas in pure form. Hers was to work with people individually who, as she said, 'already knew what they wanted.'

When she left the Prieuré in 1929, Gurdjieff gave her a MS copy of *Beelzebub's Tales* with the words, 'Go and help your husband in London.'

For this purpose she organized a House for Work based on the principles laid down at the Prieuré. Here some people could live, others visit.

To show people what they actually were and to fight on the side of the 'eternal against the temporal' was a task that aroused little gratitude in unprepared people or in those who defended and protected their little selves whose very life was threatened. But to those who really wished to see themselves—to see what IS—she gave inestimable help.

I was present at her reunion with Gurdjieff at Mendham in 1948. It was as though they had never been apart. And because I was with her, he gave me some experiences that after the passage of thirty years are still vividly present.

During this, his last visit to U.S., Gurdjieff told Madame Ouspensky: 'I need you to help me in my work for the next ten years.' He himself died the following year but she carried out his wish to her own final illness—just over ten years later.

Dorothy Darlington

EDITOR'S NOTE

In Madame Ouspensky's successive houses near London and later at Mendham, New Jersey, Saturday evenings were reserved for a particular purpose.

It was then that she would speak of the Ideas. But she did not give lectures. This book records some of her talks—many verbatim and others, particularly those of 1945, pieced together from notes that she corrected. Nothing has been added and, where possible, her own Anglo-Russian idiom has been preserved.

Where repetition occurs it is and was deliberate. Madame herself called it, 'beating on the same point.' It must also be remembered that the talks were addressed to different people on different occasions and at different times.

1945

It is time to start work.
Enough talking.
What is work?
How to work? How to start?

Work is a definite effort directed to
a definite aim. But which aim?
For us, development of consciousness—
change from one level to another
which is higher. A man is only with us
if he has this aim.

For work, organization is needed
because man cannot work alone.
What does an organization mean?
It means putting definite limitations on people.
Each person in it has a place
and a definite function to fulfil.

'Place' is determined by specific gravity.
No one can give a man his place or take it away.
It depends on valuation of the work—
the extent of valuation.

Is a man's valuation really for the work
or is it personal, for himself?

These evenings can only be useful if you remember
their purpose. The purpose is self-examination.
You are not here for a lecture or idle talk.
It is no good coming as an audience.

Self-examination means finding our position relative
to this work...what we know and what we don't know,
what we have concluded, what we have really taken
from the System—have accepted or not. Whether
we want to begin. Whether we have aim and want
to change. Or whether, perhaps, we are here by
mistake—have come into the wrong shop.

How much, after so many years,
have we really accepted? It seems we avoid thinking
so as not to see where we stand.

It is necessary to start. And our common aim
should be consciousness. What leads to it?
What prevents it? Self-examination can show us.

Sleep prevents it—turning thoughts, imagination,
ego and so on. It is only possible to gain
consciousness as much as we go against these.
One is at the expense of the other.

We need to learn which of our features are harmful
to our work and which lead toward our aim.
If we inner consider, are envious or critical,
it is obvious where these lead.
So our reactions and actions place us.
They show our position relative to work.

Don't judge others.
Examine yourself.
For this, deep self-sincerity is needed.

We have asked what leads to consciousness
and what prevents it. We need to understand that
nothing is static. A man changes every moment.
So he must question himself every moment, where
he stands, which way he moves. He must ask himself
who speaks, who acts, who reacts.

The characteristic of sleep is that everything
happens. It goes by itself, drifts, slides.
This is the fundamental point:
everything goes without effort.

Should we allow ourselves every indulgence?
How absurd! Then we only slide downhill.

With effort, we can climb a mountain.
But not just any effort. It has to be right effort.
Effort directed toward aim.

Three of Gurdjieff's aphorisms were read:

Number 6: *Here we can only direct and create conditions, but not help.*

Number 7: *Know that this house can be useful only to those who have recognized their nothingness and who believe in the possibility of changing.*

Number 5: *Remember you came here having already understood the necessity of struggling with yourself—only with yourself. Therefore thank everyone who gives you the opportunity.*

No man can be helped unless he helps himself. Because everything depends on his own effort. The right result can only come through struggle, fight. A man cannot expect it to come by itself.

We need to review the conclusions so far: People may sit in the same room, live in the same house. But only those with a common aim are 'together'.

And what is our aim?

Presumably, to change our level of being. To develop consciousness, come to the highest. We believe this is possible. So we accept we are not as we should be. This is the basis of all teachings, all religions.

Whoever accepts the same truths and principles is with us— 'together'. Those who do not accept are not in the work— automatically do not belong.

So where do we stand? Are we in the work? On the circumference? Or outside? We need to examine ourselves all the time. Our reactions and attitudes place us.

Next, effort is needed—to fight what opposes our aim. Without effort, nothing can come. Everything must be earned. For this, it is also necessary to have determination. And persistence.

The question is what to fight? We need to fight what
opposes our aim. That is, if we have an aim.

The first obstacle is imagination. We live in imagination
all the time. It is unprofitable because based on
nothing real, like a bubble. While it exists, we see, hear,
understand nothing. It prevents us perceiving reality.

Imagination is in thoughts. In dreams. In identification.
In negative emotions. All are based on imagination,
all lead away from reality.

They may seem innocent enough at the time.
Yet, for us, they are neither small nor insignificant.
Because they lead to the devil or evil. What 'evil'?
Constant leakage of energy.

Self-remembering needs energy. Work on attention
needs energy. Man only lives when he has the energy to
stand apart from himself and not to be lost in dreams. So
energy must be saved. It is like saving money for buying
something.

Man is not given free will. But he is given free choice.
We can choose. Man is what he chooses.
We place ourselves by our choice—not by dreams
or vague intentions.

It is a fight. A fight for what shall have power over us.
Where the power is, we are. We have two forces in us—
positive and negative. The third force, the balance,
is lacking.

What is work in our ordinary lives?
Definite effort for a definite purpose.
What is needed for this, for our ordinary work?
What things are required?

We need to realize work is necessary.
And need to know how to do it. We need a method,
practice, experience. A standard we can refer to
throughout. A plan to remember. Continuity, step
by step. Preparation for difficulties that will come.
Intelligence. Application of mind—to remember
the main purpose and avoid becoming either
distracted or engrossed or lost in detail. We need
an interest, an attitude of warmth. Skill. Right tools.
Right materials.

Exactly the same things are necessary in our work.

Results show the differences between talk or
intentions and doing. Facts are what count,
not psychology.

Mistakes happen because we are not clear
what work is, what to work for. Aim is not
formed yet and cannot be formed before
we realize what we lack.

Presumably our common aim is development
of consciousness. Right and wrong exist relative
to that. Right is what helps aim. Wrong is what
hinders.

Conditions are created for people who already
have aim, who know they have nothing, who know
they need help. The purpose of organized work is to
help people to study themselves and to be able
to remember themselves. But not every effort is
work. Work means right effort—effort according
to aim.

If people forget their own aim, then the means
is taken for the end.

We are sleepwalkers—asleep all the time.
We live in dreams and imagination.
We do not understand that sleeping man is in chaos.
He starts one line, changes, starts another...
For, by law, all lines decline, change direction.
Organization is needed to give man the shocks
that make the line of work possible.

We need to recognize in ourselves which
characteristics and tendencies lead toward sleep
or consciousness. But we change constantly.
Nothing is static. We need to watch the whole time
to see who we are.

We have different levels in us—and higher levels
do not come by themselves. They are reached only to
the extent that we work and struggle against our sleep.
It is a question of choice. We are what we choose—
not what we think about ourselves, dream or intend.

If a man likes his sleep and considers it natural,
he cannot work. Work only starts when he knows
what he wants and why. The rest is only preparation.

Try to remember why Saturday evenings started and where the talks have led. We spoke about the need for self-examination. We cannot start from illusion.

We think we understand because we use the words of the System freely. For instance, we use the word 'work'. But we have no idea what work is.

Work is very far from us. We have not even started to work. We deceive ourselves. But everything is according to law. What we sow, we reap.

And so we find we have no aim and have not yet accepted the main ideas of the System.
Surely the question is still: how to start work?

1946

Try to reconstruct what all these conversations
have been about, the connection between them and
where they lead. They were not started to occupy
time or for amusement. Empty words lead nowhere.
Understanding is necessary.

For example, what does the word 'work' mean?

Our System shows that man is a machine, has no I,
no will, cannot do, that everything happens to him.
He is asleep.

How many people, do you think, realize this after
going to lectures for so many years? Because as much
as a man really understands this idea, he begins to hate
his state. Desire grows in him to come out from it,
to acquire what he has not. He wishes to be—
to remember himself.

Have we real desire to be? A definite aim?
Or are we full of contradictory desires?
Is everything changeable in us?
Has nothing formed yet?

For aim exists only as long as you remember it and
make effort to attain it. It presupposes presence of
knowledge, mind and desire. It presupposes one
who directs it. Aim is to be free from the law of
mechanicalness.

Where aim exists, everything is judged by it.
It becomes your indicator and your guide.
With aim, there exists right and wrong.
Man begins to discriminate what is profit for him
and what is loss.

For man, there exists only what he perceives. But man is divided into two categories: he who believes what he sees and feels and he who is critical of what he sees and feels—who has some objective truth.

The function which compares, judges and draws conclusions is reason. For example, the senses tell man the horizon is the edge of the world. But reason, helped by knowledge and the experience of others tells him this is not so. By reason, man distinguishes what is useful or not. What he can allow or must forbid himself. He comes to valuation.

For what does it mean that man is a self-creative being? Not that he can do. He is a medium through which different influences pass—A, B and C.
One man takes everything on the same level.
Another can distinguish the difference in levels.
A man who recognizes the difference in levels can choose which influence he will be open to and accept. By being receptive to higher influences, the medium itself becomes changed.

So, by his reaction, man places himself—shows his degree of consciousness. One who blames circumstances or others for everything shows himself to be a fool. One who questions himself, mistrusts his reactions, is in a different position.

Man is created up to a certain point to serve nature's purpose. But to get something for himself depends on a different part of him—a part of that does not work yet and has to be created. Development is against the current, against lower laws, against nature. What is natural is what happens. But struggle against what happens, struggle to discriminate happening from doing, struggle to make order in oneself, is the direction of development.

Man is a machine created by nature to serve nature's purpose. In the mass, such machines provide food for the moon. They have no meaning as individuals.

What are the characteristics of a machine?
It works involuntarily, without choice.
It has to work as its maker designed it: a tractor must pull weights, a coffee grinder must grind coffee. The human machine must eat, breathe, talk, move, love. A machine works as a result of impulses given from outside. The starter of a tractor is pushed, the handle of a coffee grinder is turned. Nature arranges that life influences play on the human machine, and it works accordingly.

How do nature's purposes make themselves felt in the machine? By the feeling of pleasant and unpleasant. Following the pleasant and avoiding the unpleasant keeps the machine working as nature requires—that is, making food for the moon.

This is 'natural'.

All this happens. And it happens according to tendencies inherent in the construction of the machine, which has to work in a certain way and no other. This is the circle of mechanicalness.

How to come out from this circle? Remember there is in the human machine the possibility of being. What does being mean? Being is conscious, voluntary, has choice. Being means the possibility of acting from within, instead of only as the result of external stimuli. Being is something which must be created beyond the point of Do 48. It does not exist yet. This is what is meant by 'man is a self-creative being'.

If man believes he is already awake, will he make effort to wake up? Change of viewpoint is needed before anything can come. Man who allows himself to believe in 'I', to feel superior, or that he is unfairly treated, can get nowhere. Because everything he does will be built on imagination not fact. The fact is that man has many 'I's', is asleep, can do nothing. Seeing this fact brings change in point of view.

Try to distinguish everything that belongs to old point of view from what belongs to the new—the old Adam from the new man. Change of point of view is what sorts people out, the sheep from the goats. Belief in 'I' belongs to Hydrogen 48.

Some things that belong to old point of view may be necessary in special circumstances. The ambassador must have pride. But there must be something which uses pride, acts it for a definite purpose. This is quite different from pride possessing a man and using him. Same Hydrogen but from different source.

What is this house for? A 'house' means conditions.
Conditions mean help. Desire for help is natural in
a man who begins to change his point of view.
If a man already knows everything, naturally he does
not need help or conditions. But one who realizes he has
nothing and is nothing needs conditions. For change two
things are necessary—great desire and right conditions.

People expect help. Who can be helped? People cannot
be helped because they do not know what they want.
It is as if you go to a shop and do not know if you want
to buy chocolates or boots. This is madness.

To take, you must already have aim. Something must
already be formed which knows good from bad, left
from right. Nothing can be given. And not everybody
can receive. He who has eyes to see, let him see.
He who has ears to hear, let him hear.

What does help mean? There can be no individual help.
Help means conditions. Madame and Mr Ouspensky
never expected help, only conditions.

For work is one's own process. Eggs need warmth
to hatch, but in themselves they are either fertile or
infertile. Growth is for very few, only for those who have
strongest desire, who fight, struggle, make super efforts.
Man cannot work unless he both knows what he wants
and has enough determination to get it.

Everything is under law. Remember the three storied factory. Up to a certain point, everything in man works by nature, for nature's purposes. Man eats, sleeps, moves, loves because these activities are part of nature's needs. All this happens. Man is a piece of meat in his lifetime, food for the moon at his death. Never forget that the earth occupies a very bad place in the universe.

Beyond this point man must strive for himself.
To be a self-creative being needs great desire.
Desire includes mind, is based on the realization of what a man needs in order to escape. Desire shows the level of origin of desire —'Who in me desires what?'
When a man feels the immense greatness of the world and his own smallness, desire to grow develops.

Someone asked about imagination. If we accept we are always in imagination, we must accept the result. This means man sleeps, is food for the moon. Our System says, as long as we allow imagination to control us, nothing can come. If you think imagination is innocent, only worse and worse can follow. It is a liar, a devil. If we know imagination, we know our enemy.

The chief characteristic of imagination is that it gives no result. It is a deceiver. You can imagine a tree—but try to get an apple off it. Not even a cow will be satisfied with imaginary food.

First it is necessary to see, then choose. Choice is between real and unreal. Which do you value? If you want something real, imagination immediately becomes poisonous.

Discrimination comes from reason. Reason shows that imagination has no foundation, shows that everything is limited by time and space. Where imagination is, nothing real can exist. We need to be on guard against imagination, to fight with it, to accept that it brings only evil results. First, attitude must change for if imagination were innocent there would be no need to fight.

Question: I took a decision without verifying. I justified the decision, and thought it was based on fact.

Answer: From this one sees the liar, the active monkey in oneself. There is no discrimination here because there is no work. No work because no aim, no fear of results, nobody on guard. The machine rushes on by its own impetus. Everything happens. The chief false idea is that anything can happen rightly. Accepting and rejecting depends on knowledge and discrimination. Only when you feel danger do you begin to fight.

Question: How can I distinguish fact from imagination?

Answer: Don't expect results so soon. Results come after a long process. You are like a small boy in the garden who digs up carrots to see if they are growing.

Remember, organized work is for people who know what they want. Aim cannot be formed without realising what we have not. Our common aim is supposedly development of consciousness, to be free from the law of mechanicalness. Right and wrong exist only in relation to that. Right is what helps in direction of aim, wrong is what hinders. Conditions are for people who have already formed their aim, who know they have nothing and need help. The conditions of organized work are to help people study themselves, to help them to be able to try to remember themselves. But not every effort is work. Work means right effort, effort in accordance with aim.

Question: I think if one really sees one's position it might bring feeling. My problem is to feel my position.

Answer: Everything depends how man looks at things, what he calls right or wrong, what he demands from himself. Has he accepted the Ideas or not? Have they germinated in him? This is what places him. Either he belongs to the category of those who want to escape or of those who are content to remain in a vicious circle. Realization depends on how you change your viewpoint, in which relation you take things.

Question: Surely the first thing is to notice what takes place in oneself.

Answer: But you cannot if you keep your old point of view. It will be accidental, with no continuity, no power, no force.

Question: One forgets that there is far less difference between sleeping and waking state than between waking state and consciousness.

Answer: Absolutely right. People keep old ideas.

Question: At times I realize my position is terrible— no control and only death ahead. But these moments don't remain.

Answer: Exactly. You can be on watch only if you feel danger ahead. Then you will be on guard. If everything is quiet you go to sleep.

Question: *Does the question of right effort enter here?*

Answer: What do you call right effort?

Question: *Doesn't everything start from trying to understand about self-remembering?*

Answer: Self-remembering depends on whether you have aim or not—not on trying.

Question: *I see continual distractions. But isn't this my material?*

Answer: There must be distractions. This is life. Remember that three forces are necessary. One pulls, another moves, but third must watch and judge.

Question: *I suppose it depends whether your interest lies in politics or in acquiring consciousness.*

Answer: Where your heart is, there your treasure is also. Man is interested in the thing near and dear to him. Everything depends on energy, on one's point of view, how one takes things, what one calls right and wrong and what one demands from oneself.

If a man believes he is already awake, will he make effort to wake up?

Everybody speaks about their own opinions. Opinions are of no interest. Does man sincerely desire to change? Is he dissatisfied with his state and longing to escape from it? Or is he content with himself as he is? It is by this criterion that men go into different barrels, different categories. Not by their opinions, which belong to personality and can never change anything.

To talk of 'Carbon 12' and other numbers is absurd. These things must be spoken of as facts, not as numbers. Someone said that they didn't understand where Carbon 12 had come from. This is comic. Madame also does not understand and had never mentioned it.

The question is, does something exist which judges impressions and reactions as they arise? Is some aim already formed which stands guard, accepting or rejecting impressions or thoughts according to whether they are helpful or harmful.

Someone else was not quite clear about Do 48. Do 48 is personality, imagination, opinions, the whole unreal structure of thought which keeps us in sleep. Is there or is there not a part which wants to see, wants to know the truth, and can therefore judge and begin to control this Do 48?

This part has to be created. People do not realize what a long process it is. They take it as something sudden and definite. Realization comes at first by flashes only. It grows gradually as the result of long process, long work.

From dissatisfaction with one's state, desire to escape grows. From desire and knowledge aim is formed. Where aim exists, everything in man is revalued and judged from this point of view. What is found to be against aim must be vigorously struggled with. This gradually appears.

Question: I don't see how to go against this terrifyingly powerful part which reduces everything to the lowest level.

Answer: Inevitably there are two forces in us which fight. This is the law of nature. It all depends whether there exists a third thing that judges, chooses, resists.

Question: What is the difference between actually seeing illusions in oneself and simply accepting the idea?

Answer: Seeing dreams depends on the degree of awareness in that moment. Awareness depends on energy accumulated in previous moments.

Question: How to have these realizations more often?

Answer: By effort, by work. Work means saving energy. Our System shows us everything is limited. Energy is limited. The question is for which purpose it is used? Self-remembering depends on how much energy is saved in reserve for this purpose. Save, and you can remember yourself. Waste, and you sleep.

To discriminate between saving and wasting, it is necessary to know right and wrong. Right use of energy is what helps you to remember aim, wrong is what prevents you.

Question: Is belief that I can change part of wrong point of view?

Answer: If there is only the machine, nothing can be done. A sense of 'I' is part of the machine, and cannot grow. But something else is possible.
Man is like a person with a very big house, who lives only in the cellar. If he begins to realize he is in the cellar and that there are better places in the house, something may begin. The desire to achieve grows from dissatisfaction.

Individual man, his position and possibility of escape, is the starting point of the System and our work. Man is simply a process. This means that change takes a long time. Nothing is possible suddenly. Man can only accept or reject. By accepting one set of influences, rejecting the other, the medium itself may eventually change.

Yet all the time we continue to speak from the point of view of 'I', of 'doing'. People think they have 'rights' because they have heard the Ideas over many years. If they don't change, they blame the System. But a process has no 'rights'. It is a miraculous privilege to have heard these ideas at all. We don't realize the miracle—we see elephants flying and think it ordinary.

Remember escape is only for the very fewest. There is no open door, no exit permit. Only a few out of millions of fish eggs are fertile. Only a few men out of millions can develop. It is only possible because, by their very smallness and insignificance, the few will not be missed. Our interest is to be among those few.

This is survival of the fittest. It means the greatest effort and longest struggle. The kingdom of heaven is taken by violence. Man who wants something very badly, sells everything else to buy it. Remember the parable of the pearl of great price. Work depends on strongest desire. It means resisting happenings, guarding the mind, trying to self-remember.

But, for this, energy must be there already. How is that possible? Only by saving, drop by drop. Only in the actual moment that you resist happenings—put a stick in the wheel—do you save energy. Then the stick breaks and the wheel turns again. Only in the actual moment of great effort is a drop of energy saved.

You cannot speak of digging or physical work as saving energy. Certainly it is better to do work that needs attention than to do nothing. But this is on a different scale.

Energy is saved only by resisting, controlling, directing. Resisting happenings, guarding thoughts, need the greatest effort and long struggle. Man's possibility is like water which drop by drop wears through stone. Persistence, perseverance, beating always on the same point.

The three storied factory shows what a machine is, what its fate must be. There is one point of escape. But think what this requires.

Only a man who really feels how desperate his position is will attempt it. Yes, we say, we want to escape from prison but in the same moment we feel it is not too bad, perhaps not really prison at all. How can a man with such feelings undertake the difficulties of escape?

One must be longing, crying.
What will one give for it? That is the test.
What will one give? What couldn't one give?
Intentional suffering, doing what personality dislikes—this is what is necessary.
Likes and dislikes mean happenings.
Resist happenings.

You don't know how little time there is.
Now is our chance. But for how long?

1947

We are not what we should be.
As long as we do not know and realize this,
we have no possibility of change.
To the degree that we realize we are not,
we have the possibility of becoming.

Change means not altering on the same level,
but being part of a different world, living under
different laws.

As we are, we cannot perceive Reality, we cannot
even imagine what Reality is like. The first real
change comes as a perception that we are not
separate individuals with separate existence.
We only exist as part of a larger whole.
Either we can belong to a growing part or else
we belong to the mass, the outer darkness
which can only increase in chaos.
This is our choice.

We need to sum up for ourselves: How is change of being possible for man and on what does this depend?

Only when aim is established can work begin and behavior become obligatory. What leads to our aim is right—what takes us away from it is wrong. We must find out what pulls us away, what hinders us.

The first thing is lack of concentration, wandering attention. If we direct attention on our aim, for how long can we keep it? Only for a very short moment because everything drags us away. By resisting we can find what drags us and see where we stumble. Where our attention is, there we are.

Because our attention is dispersed we have no unity, we do not exist. We consist of many small, separate I's. In order to direct attention we need energy which we do not have because we waste it all the time. We have to collect this energy drop by drop.

We fritter our energy on small things—have nothing left for important ones. If we spend all our money on chocolates, we cannot buy boots. What we are able to get is in proportion to what we can save.

Work means directed attention, always toward aim. Only directed attention gives observation.

Question: It seems to me that one should first take the furthest aim and then find landmarks toward that. Is that right?

Answer: Everything depends, if you really have an urgent reason to move or only think you want to go and don't yet know where, why or for what. You cannot move anywhere if you don't know where you want to go and have no reason to move. You will only walk in circles. It is also not only a question of knowing where one wants to go but having the urgency and reason to leave the place where on is. This is why it is necessary for man to see what he lacks before he can have the desire to seek it. Only if you know where you want to go can landmarks be useful for you, because then they show which direction to avoid and which to follow.

Question: The problem seems to be how to create enough energy.

Answer: It should already be clear to you that we cannot create energy. We can only save energy, stop wastage. This is possible only if it is your heart's desire and only as long as you know what you want.

Question: On my way here for an hour and a half I tried hard to stop turning thoughts. I would catch them for a moment and stop them but then they would go on again. I don't see what can be done about them.

Answer: What could be expected from an hour and a half of effort? Is achievement so near? In work, as in everything, achievement can only be reached through perseverance and patience. If you expect quick results, it means you do not realize yet the forces you have to fight against. Man is able to do only in the moment, as long as he has the desire and memory to fight with these forces.

It is only possible if you put stick in wheel. The stick will be broken but a drop of energy will be saved. And energy can only be saved drop by drop, by accumulation. You again discuss what is what instead of finding out how to escape. If it does not lead us to our aim, it becomes wise-acreing.

Think what makes the dividing line between mankind— between the man who walks in a vicious circle and the man who tries to escape from it, wants to change the level of his being.

.

Everything depends on how man looks at himself, what he expects and what he demands from himself. This shows to which category he belongs.

Man in the work already realizes he has different levels in himself. He becomes according to how he behaves. He already sees the connection between cause and effect. He sees danger in his reactions and sees the necessity of discrimination. He sees the need to be on guard, to fight with his lowest self. Whereas ordinary man accepts everything in himself as inevitable, man in the work demands from himself behavior according to his creed. For him, truth exists.

Our aim is to free ourselves from the law of mechanicalness—which is our devil—in order to be able to remember ourselves. In accordance with this aim, everything that frees us is good, everything that enslaves us is bad.

Here, in order to work, we need to know what is right, what is wrong. Man has no idea of this. He needs new knowledge, new attitudes, a new outlook. But if it is the same old person who struggles, who keeps the same valuations, nobody can help him. He has a relative approach. The same thing at one moment is right, at another moment is wrong. There is no way out of it and that is why we need a point to which all our attention is fixed.

What is our objective? Consciousness. It can only be our objective if we see how unconscious and asleep we are. If we do not realize we are asleep, we can never be conscious.

That is why it is necessary to start with obstacles. One must know sleep not as theory but as fact.

Work is struggle and fight—warfare with oneself. So, one must know what is right and what is wrong. Man can do nothing. It is only in the moment when he remembers that he can do.

The question is how to start work.

People are too overloaded with material. They cannot digest what they have. They must now examine themselves to find what they really know and what they don't know—and not mix them together. But they must start with what they know.

Because work must be based on facts, not on imagination, not on words. If identification is a fact for you, when you begin to lose yourself you realize that harm is done to yourself. Then you can start work. If you think it is all nonsense, that it has no consequence—there is no question of work. This is the tragedy. Because as long as a man has an objective and knows what he wants, everything is judged by how it affects his aim. There is a division into useful and harmful.

It all depends on what we value, how we look at things, what we want. According to that, results come—and not according to what we say.

If you want to work, if you want self-remembering, you must realize you cannot remember your self—except for a second. You need intentionally to fix attention on a definite idea and hold it as long as possible. For that moment, struggle to keep attention on the idea 'I want to be'—or however you put it. Fix attention on the idea 'I don't want to be what I am. I don't want to be a machine.'

Man must know the difference between one state and another. He must like one and hate the other. If he sees those states as equal, nothing comes. Then, man must know why he wants to be different. He must experiment and see the difference. He must try to make himself remember, even out of curiosity, in order to have material to compare.

The System gives us new ideas, a new outlook,
a new teaching. It shows us what is what, why
a thing is good or bad and how to look at things.
If a man justifies all the time, lies, and does not
see the harm in it, nothing can be changed.
He will remain forever crystallized and nothing
more. The crystallization merely becomes stronger.
If things do not go up, they go down. Nothing is
static. Either you advance or fall back. You must
remember the law of seven—everything moves
every moment—either involves or evolves.
Growth or degeneration.

People must come to laws. They must look on
themselves as machines under law. Then the
question is how to escape. There is only one way.
If you accept this idea, you will wish. If you don't
accept this principle and do not wish, nothing can
be done.

This work is not for everybody. It is for people
who really believe—who can perceive its truth.
It is not for those who take it as words or as some
interesting study. This house is not for people
who study theory but for those who wish to work
on themselves—for those who accept the fact that
they are sleeping people.

Again conversation goes round in a circle because people talk without accepting fundamentals.

Questions show that people do not accept they are machines, are asleep, have no I, no will and that everything just happens to them.

This is shown, for instance, in the question: 'When we try to discriminate in ourselves who speaks, does it help to think of it from the angle of functions?'As if it were possible in ordinary sleep to study or discriminate. Study comes after observations which give new material, and observations cannot be made in sleep. It must not be forgotten, our aim is consciousness. In as much as we have consciousness we can study functions.

Our aim is to try to remember ourselves always and everywhere. The mistake is in thinking we are able to do in sleep. In order to try to awake we must first go against our mechanicalness.

We need to watch constantly to see who we are. We have different levels. The higher are reached only to the extent that we strive. They do not come by themselves.

Everything is relative and depends on what it is related to. For man, everything is related to his point of view.

Ordinary man's point of view is based on error, on illusion. It is the product of his imagination and is contradicted by facts. The system relates man to facts, which man can verify for himself. Ordinary man considers he has unity, that he has 'I', he is able to do, is conscious, has will, is a man. The work shows man has no I but many contradictory I's. He has no oneness, no controlling center. Everything happens with him. He cannot do. He is asleep. He has no consciousness, no will. He is a machine. Between these two classes of beings there is nothing in common. Everything is opposite.

Ordinary man is satisfied with himself. He has no urge to change. He acts before he thinks, because nothing is formed yet which can discern or discriminate. He does not see the necessity to give account of and control himself. He does not know himself. He does not see that he lives in illusion and chaos. In order to start to work, man must be dissatisfied with himself, must see his own limitations and have the urge to escape from his prison. As much and as often as man realizes he is asleep and that everything depends on his state of consciousness, consciousness will become his aim.

There were questions last week about different levels. For the ordinary meaning of words we can look in the dictionary. But we cannot start from ABC. From the System's point of view, words have definite meaning. We are reminded of the different worlds in which man lives, of the different laws that come from different levels in the Ray of Creation and of the Table of Hydrogens. The Table of Hydrogens shows us the descent of finer matters into coarser. It shows that all levels of materiality, of different density, are within us, coming from different places. And if we remember the Food Diagram, we can see how these different levels of materiality are physical things. A box of matches is on one level, impressions are on another. Ordinary impressions are hydrogen 48. All other possibilities are represented by hydrogens 24 and 12.

JOTTINGS FROM A NOTEBOOK

How to find real I and self knowledge?

You find something which is 'not I'. Later this
becomes ordinary I and you find something else
that is 'not I'. You cannot jump at once to real I.

We live only in formatory and lower parts of centers.
If we live in that world we only turn and turn and
become more set.

To see mechanicalness in oneself and others from
System point of view means also to see way out.
To see oneself makes one happy because only then
can one hope to change.

Lack of unity and distortion do not come from
without but from within the organization. It comes
through personal opinions of people with no unity
of understanding of Ideas.

Attention needs food. And its food is what we have
achieved. [what experience we bring to it]

There is the attention of Man 1, 2, 3, 4, 5, 6 and 7.
It depends on who we are. Attention is like light.
It is in all centers.

It is impossible to take ourselves as existing separately and not in relation to the whole.

X has many devils. They stronger than they used to be so necessary to have stronger reason to oppose them. Not means doing but being constantly on guard. Two streams have met and are in turmoil. While turmoil lasts, do not think. You cannot quieten it by thinking. Thinking processes comes from the other—as result. Not the other from thinking.

You used to believe that personality could achieve. This is gone. If you start from realization that you are a machine, that you do not remember yourself, you will be on guard and begin to control. All struggle is against imagination. If 'it' sees, it is imagination that sees.

Nothing is possible if we start from wrong point of view—if we think of ourselves as existing and as complete. We are in the world so that we can complete ourselves.

Necessary think which questions and problems we have and what is important or not.

About 'I am' and 'not I': Everything that shows up is 'not I'. We do not know what to look for or where to look. At the same time 'I' exists somewhere. Necessary not fantasy and not become dead. Important thing is to learn not to trust oneself.

Mr Gurdjieff is our future. We are his past.

EXTRACT FROM A LETTER
TO MR OUSPENSKY IN 1919

...I would like to tell you about my latest observations, but I am not sure I shall be able to. I used to ask you the question: where are efforts leading to? Having surmounted one obstacle one is faced with a series of other insurmountable ones. This gave rise to the thought: what is the good of efforts if in the final result they do not lead anywhere? I wrote to you that Gurdjieff used to say that no effort is ever lost, that energy remains. Now I became convinced through experience that this is so. These last days I understood more about centers and about the difference (which nobody succeeded in defining before) between the formatory apparatus and the centers. We used to define it by saying that the formatory apparatus has no creative power and Gurdjieff used to say that it was so and yet not so. Now it appears that it has no growth and its creative power manifests itself only in a series of combinations on the same level. But of growth there is none, there is no fertilizing principle. This is why words without deeds are dead; a living word fertilizes and gives rise to growth.

It is difficult to express all this in a letter. But somehow I now understand more about the difference between centers. Now it is clear why the moving center is more conscious than the formatory apparatus. Moving center is the center of atoms. Formatory apparatus is our personality—it is the monkey that knows everything and distorts everything. This is why we must conquer our false personality, because we manifest ourselves through it...

I have formulated my wish: I want to see and I want to broaden out. At present we are all frozen and the majority of us do not even feel it.

DICTATED MESSAGES—1948

This house is only for those who have come to work on themselves and are grateful for being given conditions to do so.

Attitudes show they still do not realize necessity to start work on themselves and that all the time they waste energy judging other people which should be used to work on oneself. After many years they have still not come to this point but continue to look at other people instead of looking at themselves, still believing in their judgement of other people instead of seeing that this is the thing in themselves they have to fight.

It is not possible to answer your letters and questions, because there is no common language between us.

Impossible to talk to heterogeneous collection of people with no common creed, speaking each his own language.

You have no creed, no formed aim, no established truth to relate everything to. And so, for you everything is arbitrary, nothing is obligatory, and there is no language possible.

You think you ask for help, but you forget even the idea of what asking for help means. Asking for help means giving up self-will. What you ask is advice how to fulfil your own plans—which themselves are built without any foundation.

And now it is your problem, to find out what you really believe in, what really exists for you, where you stand, where you intend to move, and with whom.

NOVEMBER 1951

I am glad people come. Only all depends on why they come, what they come with and what do they hope to get. Because people can get in accordance with what they understand. Without right approach right result cannot be achieved.

Each organization requires order and discipline because, without order and discipline, everything becomes chaos.

MESSAGE TO HOUSE ON OCTOBER 30TH, 1949

Mr Gurdjieff died. Only for us he is not dead.

Before he died he gave us so much of ideas, this puts us under obligation to try to repay.

Man's life is about 80 years. Ideas live for thousands. We believe Mr Gurdjieff's ideas will live.

Now is the time to examine ourselves and to find what we received.

As he himself wrote a short time ago:

'After 50 years of preparation and having overcome
the greatest difficulties and obstacles, I have
now reached the moment when I have decided
to begin to actualize the plans I have prepared
for the transmission of my ideas to the whole of
contemporary and future humanity.

'In order to accomplish this task, I shall need the
help of all those who have understood something of
the value of my ideas and especially those who have
gained personal benefit and help from their study.'

APPENDIX

MADAME OUSPENSKY

A brief biography

Sophie Grigorievna Ouspensky was born Sophie Grigorievna Volochine—reputedly in 1874 in Kharkoff, Ukraine. At 16 she married a student with whom she had a son who was later killed, and a daughter. She divorced the student, married a mining engineer and travelled with him to remote areas in Russia.

She was introduced to Gurdjieff in 1916–17 by P. D. Ouspensky and became a member of the St. Petersburg group.

When Gurdjieff went to Essentuki in February 1918, Madame Ouspensky joined him along with scores of fellow students. When Gurdjieff left for Tiflis, Georgia, the following year, she and her daughter stayed in Essentuki with P. D. Ouspensky. In February 1920, they journeyed to Constantinople.

Ouspensky left for London in August 1921 but she stayed with Gurdjieff, later accompanying him to Germany and then to Avon, France, where in October 1922 he established his Institute at the Prieuré.

That year, Gurdjieff twice visited Ouspensky's pupils in their hired premises at Warwick Gardens.

Ouspensky's last visit to the Prieuré was in 1924. By then, he had decided that he could no longer work with Gurdjieff. Around that time Gurdjieff told Madame Ouspensky that her husband needed her in England. She loathed England and took an apartment in Asnières, near Paris where she stayed till 1927. There, London pupils visited to aid her with translations of her husband's books and formed a Work group under her direction.

Gurdjieff sent her to visit and support Ouspensky in the summer of 1928. She returned to study further with Gurdjieff, visiting England for part of the summer months only. When Ouspensky began his London lectures she was again sent off to assist him. Between 1934 and 1940, he held weekly meetings with questions and answers.

During this time, she and Ouspensky had separate quarters in various country houses. These houses, such as High Wycombe near Kent, were Madame Ouspensky's domain and the activities were far from theoretical. Physical labor combined with practical esoteric study mirrored the activity at Fontainebleau. After being dispatched by Gurdjieff a number of times to help her husband in London, she finally stayed in the UK, taking over the practical work of his groups, but kept in touch with France.

In 1931, she took a house called The Dell at Sevenoaks while Ouspensky still lectured in London. After her final move to the UK in 1931 she taught at Lyne Place in Surrey, supervising practical work, the Movements and, on occasion, readings from comparative systems such as the sayings of the Buddha, Rumi and and the *Philokalia*.

In 1931 *A New Model of the Universe* was published resulting in many new followers. And, in 1938, Ouspensky established a larger London base in Colet Gardens that could accommodate several hundred people. But, by then, the formidable Madame Ouspensky—a mixture of ferocity, strength and poise—was suffering Parkinson's disease and confined mostly to bed.

In January 1941, with the Germans occupying France and bombing London, Ouspensky felt that the Work would have a better chance of being preserved in the USA. He and Madame left for America. His lectures in New York that summer attracted few people but attendance grew.

In 1942 the Ouspenskys established a school at Franklin Farms in Mendham, New Jersey. Ouspensky spent much of his time in New York lecturing and writing, while Madame supervised the Mendham community. Though confined to bed, she still directed activities and taught her students about the fundamental principles of practical work on themselves. She placed much value on the Movements and practical work and saw that they were taught both at Lyne Place and at Franklin Farms.

Ouspensky, by then in poor health, gave his last New York lectures in 1946 and returned to the UK in 1947. He gave his final meetings at Colet Gardens and urged Madame to sell Lyne Place.

When P. D. Ouspensky died in 1947, Madame Ouspensky advised both the London and American students to go to Gurdjieff in Paris. Some, because of the war and the ban Ouspensky had placed on speaking of Gurdjieff, were not even aware he was alive. Among those she told were John Pentland and Christopher Fremantle.

When Gurdjieff visited New York in the winter of 1948 he went to see Mme Ouspensky at Franklin Farms. She showed him a chapter of Ouspensky's manuscript, *Fragments of an Unknown Teaching*, and asked if it should be published. Gurdjieff instructed her to publish it, but only after his own book *Beelzebub's Tales to His Grandson* had appeared. She published the book in America under the title *In Search of the Miraculous*. She also supervised the publication of P. D. Ouspensky's *The Fourth Way*, which appeared in 1957.

She led the work at Mendham until her death.

J. G. Bennett said:

'Of all the many remarkable people I have met in my
life, Madame Ouspensky stands out uniquely for her
singleness of purpose and her unwavering pursuit
of her aim.... She would never undertake anything
beyond her own understanding and powers.... She said
of herself: "Madame is not a teacher. She always looks
upon herself as a nursery governess who prepares
children for school."

'She is very ill, suffering from an incurable illness,
but those of you who have known her will have known
what a great power she had and with what singleness
of heart and understanding she did everything. When
I went to America, I found her even more worthy of
respect and love than she had been when I had last
seen her, seven or eight years earlier.'

Kenneth Walker wrote:

'Madame Ouspensky, who took a more and more prominent part in her husband's work after the year 1924, possessed a special gift for seeing below the surface and revealing to us what she had discovered there. She sometimes likened our personalities to large hot-air pies which we were carrying about with us very carefully in the hope that they would be duly admired. Her allegory was a particularly appropriate one, for the crust of a hot-air pie is so thin that the slightest knock from someone else will cause it to crumble, and thus reveal to the world the emptiness within.'

John Pentland recalled:

'Madame was one of those people who emanate
a force which makes them seem larger than they
actually are. She was regarded by us all as an
independent source of teaching.

    'Her instruction was direct, quite free of
moralization and expressed in bad English, relieved
by humor and much laughter at the absurdity of our
behaviour toward each other and toward herself.

    'Madame—she was always called simply
Madame—was constantly arranging conditions—
whether through physical labor on the farm, through
her carefully formulated questions and messages
to us, or through talks as we sat on the floor in her
bedroom, which had the effect of miraculously
renewing our zest and energy for living at the expense
of the ugly and sleepy associations inside us.

    'When we felt that renewal, she did not merely
tell us to observe and record how it had appeared but
confronted us with this question: 'What do you want?'

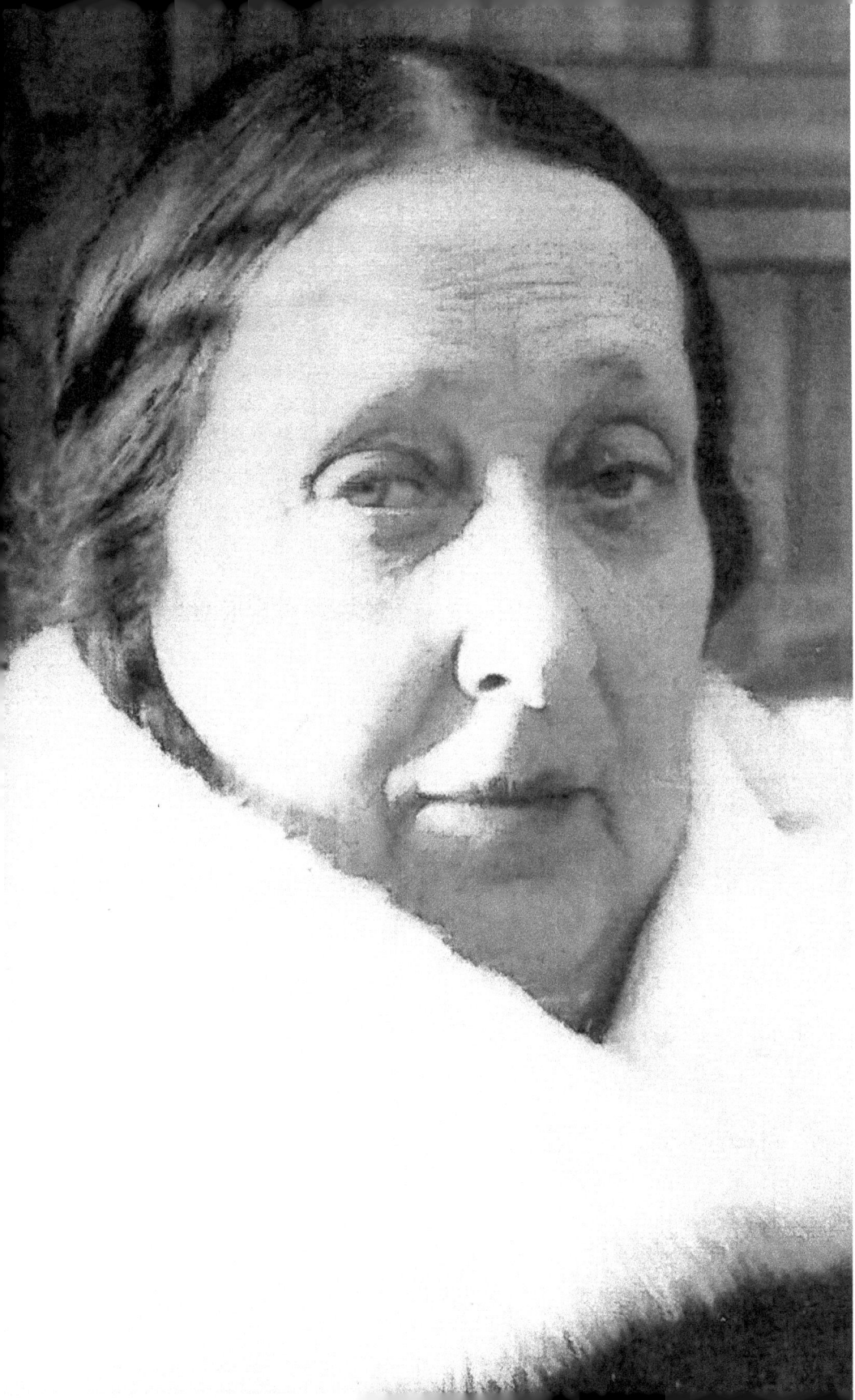

SOPHIE OUSPENSKY

from Irmis Popoff's book,
Gurdjieff: His Work On Myself, With Others, For The
Work *(1969) New York: Vantage Press, pp. 111–119*
Copyright © 1969 Irmis B. Popoff

One fateful evening, when he was lecturing in the Grand Ballroom at Steinway Hall, Mr. Ouspensky dropped a bombshell by announcing to us his decision to discontinue his lectures in New York and to return to London in the very near future.

"Those of you who go to Mendham," he said, "will have Madam Ouspensky to direct you. Those of you who do not, must find your own bearings."

That was all. As simple and as final as that!

Grief, astonishment, disbelief, desperation—all this was reflected on the faces of the persons in the Hall who felt the value of the Work that Mr. Ouspensky had been conducting here in New York. As for those of us who were not going to Mendham at that particular time— we wriggled, panted, and gasped for air in a frantic effort to save ourselves from despair. There was among us a handful who had been working closely with Mr. Ouspensky in New York whom he referred to as "his people," mentioning that those who went to Mendham were "Madam's people."

Now, these few people were more "his people" because of their attitude toward him than because he had in any way chosen them. They were always ready to serve him, to come as close to him as he permitted, to work for him; they took all he had to give according to their individual preparation, and tried to help him in ordinary practical ways such as writing reports, typing, making telephone calls, talking with people who came to the lectures for the first time, and so forth. The small services we thus eagerly rendered him added a wealth of opportunities for us to work on ourselves, to the boon that we were receiving in exchange.

We were the people he had pushed, verbally lashed, abused, annoyed, banged about; the people who, he no doubt knew, respected, loved and tried to understand him as best they could. The people who, when he was at his worst as a task maker, felt that he was at his best trying to baffle them for the purpose of helping them to sharpen their wits, to learn to think on their feet, to be impartial and to discover how to swallow in order to become strong.

It was my good fortune to be among these people. Yet his departure left me at a disadvantage. I tried to return to Mendham, but Madam did not permit it. It is quite possible that others from my group had the same experience, but I do not know. For myself, I blessed Madam for the wisdom of her decision even when I felt more at a loss in the days that followed, knowing that the miracle was over and assuming that this was the end for me since I never thought it would be possible to go on with the Work outside the general group.

I must explain here that I had gone to Mendham previously, and had come into contact with Madam Ouspensky. When she saw me for the first time she classified me on the spot as "the emotional Mrs. p. with nothing in her head." As I heard her words I had to admit that she was right, for from the very moment my eyes rested on her I felt that I loved her. My heart had leapt as though I had recognized her! I was emoting at the time, so this perception had nothing to do with reason. Perhaps the reaction was the result of the fear

I had felt before meeting her because many described her as a "monster" in disguise, always ready to pounce purringly upon those who came to the big house and torture and taunt them. It seemed she had sensed my emotion.

However, my work with Mr. Ouspensky had conditioned me. I knew he was kind and understanding, even when he appeared to be at his worst. I knew from experience that he hit hard in order to save; that he wounded in order to heal, and so I took it for granted that Madam did as much. And I was correct.

In their team it was she who worked most on the emotional side of man. Her tactics were different, but the aim and the method were the same. And because my mind had accepted and understood, I felt full of grateful admiration for her and for the Work. It was impossible to undergo such emotional transformations as I underwent, to see others undergo them, without feeling in the depths of one's being the sacred sentiments of gratitude and love on witnessing the colossal sacrifice of personality by Mr. Ouspensky and Madam Ouspensky in order to help others to stop being machines and to become men and women worthy of their Creator.

It was an unbelievably difficult task. Madam made herself expressly disagreeable, reprimanding, aping, debunking, abusing, and unmasking everybody. Yet I realized, within the limits of my experience in any event, she always was a mirror of justice and never accused anyone wantonly or unjustly except for reasons of a much higher order than were apparent to others who were not involved in the little plays in which she would call upon this or that more advanced pupil to act impromptu for the benefit of the newcomers. She found the exact sore spot in one's makeup; always exposing sham, false personality, pride, vanity, conceit, forever attacking weakness and stupidity; she was as tart and acid in her talk as she was wise and profound in her judgment.

Madam's impact on the people who came to her for the first time was much deeper than that which Mr. Ouspensky made in equal circumstances. It is possible that when we came to her we knew what to expect, and came in fear of being torn apart or wishing to be torn apart and to have, perhaps, the first real look at ourselves. One approached Madam emotionally, either loving her or hating her, but there was no feeling of admiration toward her such as Mr. Ouspensky inspired; at least not among those I knew. Not to begin with, in any event. And yet, it was she who sacrificed herself daily for the sake of those within reach of her help! It was she who ran the risk of becoming a real shrew, and of losing her way in the bargain; she who could expect nothing but resentment from those she so lavishly helped. It was, however, a resentment that was short-lived in the hearts of those who stood their ground, because eventually one came to feel—just as one came to understand with one's mind in dealing with Mr. Ouspensky—that her heart was immense and she mothered us all, having undertaken the Herculean task of weaning us away from sham. And in carrying through her task she was constantly exposed to the danger of losing everything she had won through hard work on herself by merely half forgetting that she was only acting.

My personal work with Madam was far too short to satisfy me, but long enough for me to profit immeasurably from the generosity with which she gave of herself. I shall never forget the moments I spent near her. I had nothing but love and admiration for this remarkable woman when I saw her riding through the gardens in her old car while we worked in the fields; or when she came to the dining room or the terrace while we ate lunch or had tea, to treat us all to her special brand of firework displays!

I can still feel the sensation that crept along my spine when I heard Madam approaching, her cane announcing her as she came closer and closer to the terrace or the dining room. Although small in stature, she loomed and towered above us all through the sheer strength and poise that radiated from her presence. When she reached the long narrow tables at which we sat, everyone remained motionless, eyes glued to one spot, simultaneously wishing to draw her attention and yet to become invisible to her. Each one of us was in readiness, conscious of her powerful presence, desperately trying to hold fast to our own shaking thread of presence, not knowing what to expect nor where the lash would fall, fastened to the spot as though held by a magnet, delighted to be there but almost wishing to take flight! And she would calmly take a seat at the head of one of the long narrow tables, surveying the assembly with extraordinarily calm and beautiful eyes; those limpid and penetrating eyes which laughed and sparkled while her tongue lashed.

It was not until years later, when I came into close contact with her Master, that I realized how much Madam received from him. From all the pupils in his original group that I have known she alone, through her presence, gave me the feeling, or rather the trace of the shadow of the feeling that took possession of my being in Mr. Gurdjieff's presence. In her power over people, in the depth of her presence, in deep magnetic appeal, in merciless humor and ready wit, in her extraordinary

61

mimicing ability, Madam, to my knowledge, was undoubtedly the one of Mr. Gurdjieff's pupils who resembled him most or imitated him best, as the case may have been.

In the all too short period of my proximity to Madam I never heard her say anything that was banal or superficial. This woman, for whom I had the strange feeling of having been waiting throughout the years long before I even knew she existed, had a profound influence on my life—this woman, who took my heart from me, and whom I, in turn, did my best to imitate so far as postures and gestures went. I cherished forever every word she spoke, and I imagine I can still hear her voice; not imparting the ideas and the knowledge that our revered Mr. Ouspensky gave us, but full of practical wisdom for use in ordinary living. The "nu" that usually preceded her words, still rings lovingly in my ears.

"Never offer more information than has been asked of you," I hear her telling me now, as she did once, when, upon asking me whether I had brought some person into the Work I waxed eloquent to explain how that person had come to join us. I can still see her as she sat at the table, telling us how she had hated herself when she was in the same position in which we found ourselves now whenever she caught herself lying.

I asked, in surprise, "Did you say hate, Madam?"

And she replied, "Yes, hate. Love is a result—it is not an aim, Mrs. P."

Madam was never brutal or cruel to me until the time came to forbid my returning to Mendham. Then she was adamant. Had I not loved her and trusted her, I should have hated her. Mendham was, at the time, the only door that I wanted to see open to me. But she knew best. Circumstances were such then that it would have been psychologically detrimental for me to be there. I like to think that she knew it, and refused me accordingly. However, I never stopped loving her. Perhaps I loved her the more for her refusal to let me be weak; and her words, every word that she ever spoke to me, never ceased to influence me. I was thus well able to accept my ban from Mendham without bitterness and without argument for I always had the feeling that Madam understood. And irrespective of external appearances, irrespective of the trend of events, I felt safe in the certainty of her strength and of her wisdom.

How often I wished I had occasion to witness an encounter between Master and pupil! I am convinced that Madam would have stood as close in stature to his shadow as it was possible for anyone to come!

DOROTHY DARLINGTON

An appreciation—
including the origin and editing of the text.

The text is an authentic transcription of talks given
by Madame Ouspensky to her group at Mendham,
derived
and assembled from material retained by Dorothy
Darlington
who wished this part of Madame's legacy to be
preserved.

Dorothy was the youngest of four children born in comfortable circumstances in Britain in 1889. Her father was a friend of Tolstoy. At the age of four she began to study the violin. She had a perfect ear for music and a French governess who spoke to her in French. Dorothy later became a concert violinist playing a Stradivarius bought by her father.

She joined the group in London at twenty-four. Shortly afterward, while working in the garden, she naively called out to Ouspensky, who chanced to ride by on his pony, 'Mr Ouspensky, how long will it be before I can remember myself?'

'Oh, about a month,' came the ironic and expedient reply.

She eventually abandoned her career and left the House at Lyne for America.

At Franklin Farms, Mendham, New Jersey, Madame O wanted someone to take charge of the kitchen. Various candidates were asked to prepare Welsh Rarebit. Madame tasted outcomes and sent them back.

DD was up till two in the morning putting meat through the sieve. When Madame O sampled her dish she said, 'That's right.'

She was put in charge of the kitchen and worked there for fifteen years. She rose at 5am, went to the market and carried whole sheep carcases on her diminutive shoulder back to the car.

While plucking chickens intentionally late one night in the silent kitchen, she had an epiphany. She said, 'Energy came, just by working there. We must do the impossible. Conditions in the old days were hard. Ideas become weakened, pass into life. But there is nothing to say that the individual should not develop—carry his own crumb of truth. Things he learns through conditions that become manifest to him—and do not depend on Madame de Salzmann, Madame O or anyone—are life.'

Once, while cooking for 200 people, she not only prepared the meal but also cooked the meatballs for next day. When Madame O reviewed the next day's menu, she told her not to worry about the meatballs. DD answered, 'But Madame, I have already cooked them.'

Madame replied, 'Why even I couldn't do that.'

Later on, while supervising the kitchen in Australia, she told us, 'You are in the kitchen for work, not to learn how to cook.'

During Madame O's final years, she was in charge of many

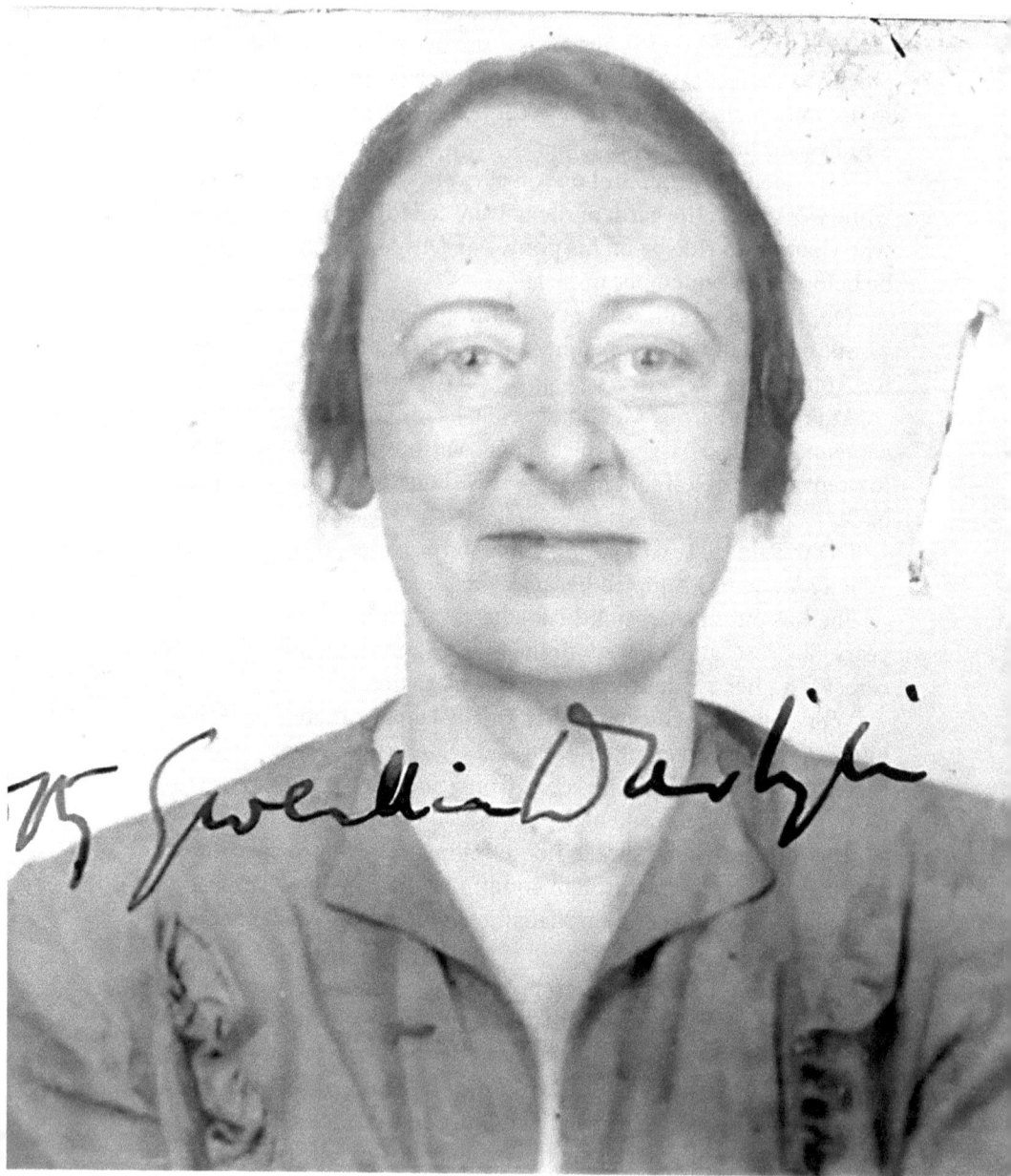

practical aspects of running the house and also co-edited *The Fourth Way*. She was present in the room when Gurdjieff visited Madame. She said, 'The expression on his face I will never forget.'

She said, 'Gurdjieff taught by his being. You learned more in an experience with him than in many conversations.'

She regarded Madame O with great reverence and affection and had decisive moments with her. Though she admitted, 'She was very hard to take. Even years later, in America, the old ones asked me what she was trying to give. They did not understand. The question is, who is interested in death?'

I took this remark as meaning psychological death., 'Surely,' I said, there is no other way?'

Dorothy replied, 'No. Not if we wish to gain anything in a single lifetime. Madame said that I was not interested in personality but only truth. That very few were like this. She said once, "I hate Dorothy Darlington. But I love you."'

She said that Madame died in her arms.

When the connection with the New York group was established she became a regular member of the Gurdjieff Foundation and, after Madame's death, went to Paris where Madame de Salzmann asked her what she wanted to do. She replied that she would leave it up to her.

In 1965, she was sent to Australia to work in tandem with George Adie (she found it impossible to work with him) and eventually mentored the Sydney/Canberra Gurdjieff Society established by C. S. Nott, aiding it through the transition from UK to American guidance during the visits of Rina Hands, Charles Wright and the initial visits of James Wyckoff. She played the piano for Movements classes, directed kitchen work, and assisted group leaders whenever help was needed.

Being radiated from her small body. The rigor of years in the early work shone through her. Those who knew her remember her enormous contribution. During the dark days of flawed hierarchy and factions in Sydney, she kept the creaking structure alive.

Her connections with overseas groups remained. Once, someone even sent her Jane Heap's couch—a huge overstuffed thing that languished in the Group House for some time until we summoned courage to sell the sacred artefact.

Dorothy was poor. She lived in a one-room serviced tenement

and supported herself to some extent as theatre critic for the *Sydney Morning Herald*, always hoping that the editors would never learn how old she was. I accompanied her to at least one production and later read her excellent and balanced review. She did much to promote theatre in this country and was a close friend of Doris Fitton who founded Sydney's Independent Theatre.

Jim Wyckoff and Dorothy worked well together. She told me, 'He was not there in the old days but he has it.' She supported us selflessly between his visits right through her eighties.

When it was known that she had terminal cancer, Madame de Salzmann summoned her back to France and they spent time together in Paris. Then Dorothy returned to Sydney where she died in 1979.

I visited her in the hospice a day or two before she died. She was still fierce and in good form. She said, 'I want a drink.'

I rushed to get her an orange juice.

She snarled, 'I said a drink.'

Mortified, I fled to the nearest pub and managed to smuggle in a bottle of scotch for her.

Dorothy was a powerful iconoclast and refreshingly deficient in vanity. At formal group functions, she would wear a red plastic net to keep her hair in place — salvaged from the netting around bulk oranges bought in the supermarket.

Her impatience with fools matched her unreserved respect for the Work. She told us that, as soon as someone said, 'I know,' you could be damned sure they didn't.

Of those who knew her, there is probably no one who did not revere her, though she once called herself, 'A bit of a bitch.'

She had in her room photographs of Mr G and Mr O and did not see Mr O as the austere man his books imply. Sometimes when she looked at his photograph, she'd cry.

So there was a deep link there.

And a profound one with Madame O.

SOURCES AND EDITING:

Dorothy had not only her own notes of Madame's Saturday evening talks but also notes of the same talks taken by up to six others. She mentions in her introduction that the notes were corrected by Madame herself.

This, then, was what she proposed we collate and edit as a group work together. Why me? Possibly because we were similar types and my work was with words.

It was a painstaking and meticulous process of comparison and evaluation, informed always by Dorothy's knowledge of how Madame spoke and how she was. As well as the precise sentence construction, we pondered long over every aspect of punctuation. Each full stop and comma was placed to represent Madame's emphatic speech pattern and uncompromising approach.

We occasionally differed over the weighting of a sentence. I'm a reasonable editor and wished the text to be balanced and strong. Dorothy, additionally, was assessing sense and authentic voice. It was a slow and difficult process, working from parallel sources. She did not wish Madame's flawed English and imperative voice to be diluted.

The result, after months of work on Sunday 'workdays' was no arbitrary collation but a long-pondered and balanced text that exactly reflects what Dorothy considered authentic and wished to present to the groups.

—CS

www.ingramcontent.com/pod-product-compliance
Lightning Source LLC
Chambersburg PA
CBHW072251110426

42742CB00039BA/2851